No Fish!

by Cathleen Rogers

FIRST EDITION

Decodable Poems

Wilson Language Training Corporation
www.wilsonlanguage.com

No Fish!

Item # WRSNF

ISBN 978-1-56778-427-5
FIRST EDITION

PUBLISHED BY:

Wilson Language Training Corporation
47 Old Webster Road
Oxford, MA 01540
United States of America

(800) 899-8454

www.wilsonlanguage.com

Copyright ©2009 Wilson Language Training.

All rights reserved. No part of this work may be reproduced or transmitted in any form or by any means, electronic or mechanical, including photocopying, recording, or by information storage and retrieval system or network, without permission in writing from Wilson Language Training Corporation.

Printed in the U.S.A.

January 2011

*To my friends in Room 160,
for your encouragement and faith*

~ Cathleen Rogers

Introduction

by Cathleen Rogers

Emergent, beginning, early, and struggling readers can all benefit from poetry. When we play pat-a-cake with our three year old, we are drawing attention to the sounds in words, thus developing the phonemic awareness that will set the stage for language acquisition. As a person learns to read, he becomes sensitive to the phonological structure of words as he begins to focus on beginning, middle, and ending sounds represented by letters and letter combinations.

I believe that these poems will add another genre to the supportive reading materials provided by Wilson Language Training. They were originally written for the younger students in Level A of the Wilson Reading System®, however, they are also appropriate as a supplemental practice for Fundations® students. While much of the text is controlled in order to practice the word structure that has been taught, many high frequency/sight words are included. With the aid of illustrations, phrased lines, and predictive rhymes, although these poems are non-controlled, we anticipate that they will be highly decodable (and enjoyable!). The poems are ideal for repeated reading, including echo and choral reading.

I'd like to thank Wilson Illustrator Leah Caracino for her wonderful illustrations.

We hope that students will be motivated to use these poems for repeated readings, memorization, and performance, which will help them to become fluent, independent readers.

Contents

Please note: These are non-controlled poems, which means the text is not limited to the taught word patterns. However, although it is not controlled, it is decodable if a student is able to accurately read 95% of the words independently.

WRS Substep*

1.1	The Fat Rat	1
1.2	Zag	3
1.3	No Fish!	5
1.4	Bess and Bill	7
1.5	Sam and Dan	7
1.6	On the Path	8
2.1	Hank, the King	9
2.2	The Run	11
2.3	The Small Colt	13
2.4	A Grand Plan	15
2.5	My Cat, Tess	16
3.1	Seven Small Kittens	17
3.2	The Dentist	19
3.3	The Class Trip	21
3.4	Fantastic Janet	23
3.5	Dennis	24
4.1	The Bike Ride	25
4.2	Camping in the Pinelands	27
4.3	Custom-Made Valentines	28
4.4	The Dog Show	29
5.1	The Tennis Pro	31
5.2	The Best Hotel	32
5.3	The Pet Rally	33
5.4	One Day Long Ago	35
5.5	Donna Apollo	36
6.1	Mrs. Yang	37
6.2	Wendy	39
6.3	Wishfulness	40
6.4	Dapple-Gray Nag	41

*See the last page for each poem's alignment with the Fundations Level and Unit.

The Fat Rat

On the mat the fat rat sat.
"A rat! A rat!" said Nat.
"Rap the rod on the mat!"
"No nap," said the fat rat.

On the mop, the fat rat sat.
"A rat! A rat!" said Matt.
"Rap the rod on the mop!"
"No nap," said the fat rat.

On the lid, the fat rat sat.
"A rat! A rat!" said Nat.
"Rap the rod on the lid!"
"No nap," said the fat rat.

On the rag, the fat rat sat.
"A rat! A rat!" said Matt.
"Rap the rod on the rag!"
"No nap," said the fat rat.

And that is how Nat and Matt
got rid of the fat rat.

NO FISH! / LEVEL A 2

Zag

Ben has a lab pup
and his name is Zag.
They run on the path
and like to play tag.

Ben said, "Let me sit
on this rock in the sun."
Zag bit his sock.
"Yip! Yip! No, let's run!"

"I will rub your neck
and pat your back.
Zag, let me check
what I have in my pack."

Ben said, "Have a sip
from this wet jug."
Zag said, "Yes! Yes!"
with a lick and a tug.

Ben said, "Have a chip
from this big bag."
Zag said, "Yes! Yes!"
with a hop and a wag.

Then Ben and Zag
went home for a nap.
Ben sat in the den
with Zag in his lap.

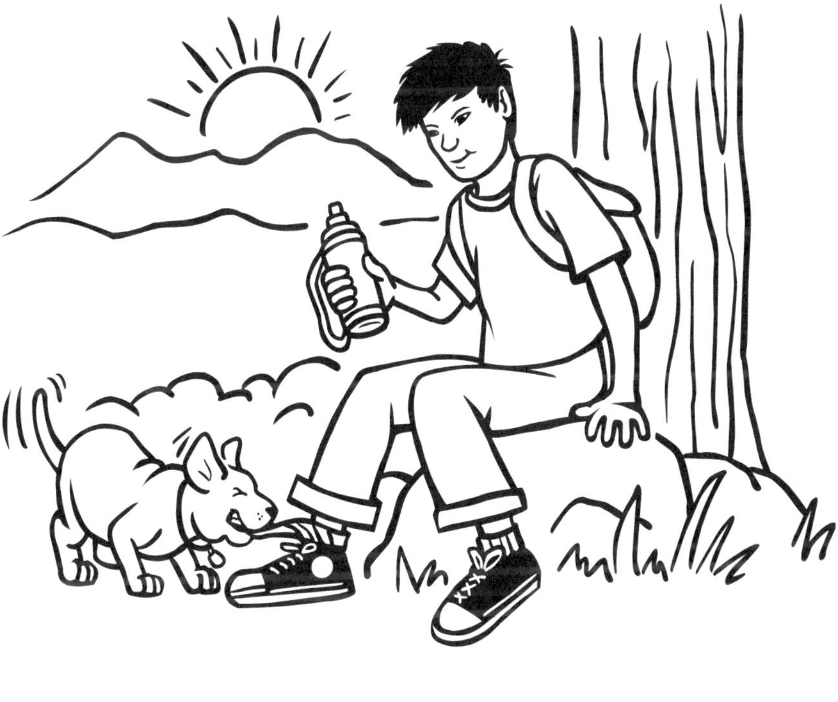

No Fish!

Rick sat on the rock and Bob sat on the dock
to fish in the red, hot sun.

Rick did hum and Bob had gum
but the fish had all the fun.

One fish bit and Rick did tug
but the fish got away with the bug.

Bob hid his net in the wet.
What did he get?
Nothing yet!

No fish on the rod!
No fish in the net!
No fish in the pan!
No fish on the dish!

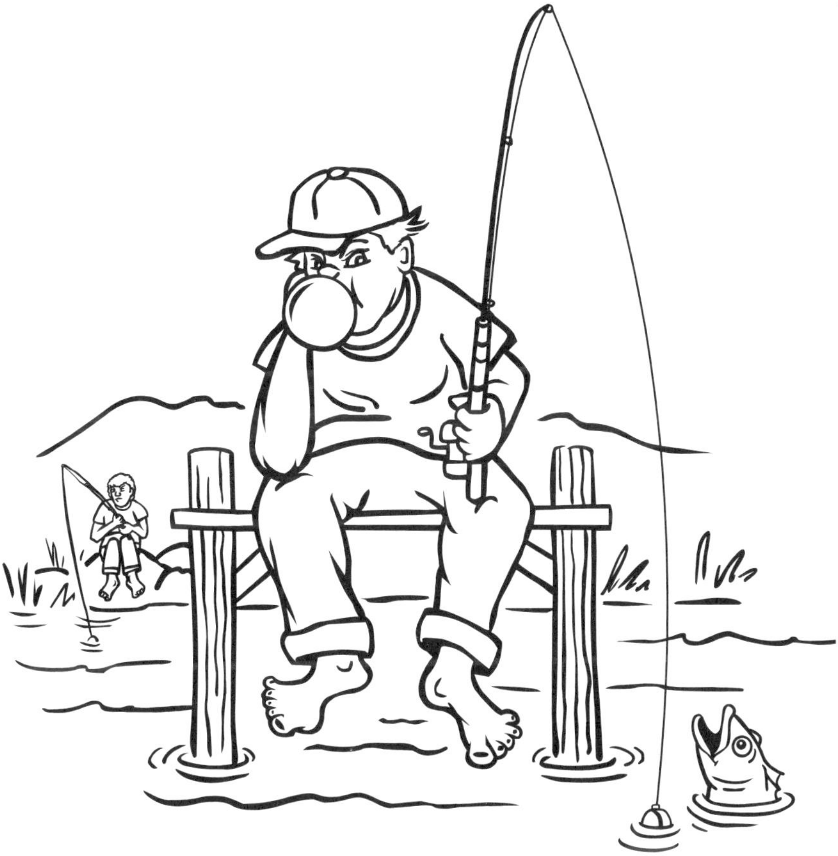

SUBSTEP 1.4

Bess and Bill

Bess sat on the wall of the well
and fell in.

Bill did pass and saw Bess fall.
He had to run to the mall to call.
Then he ran back to the well.
To Bess he did yell and yell.

A tall cop got the lass
who fell into the well.

Bess was then ill with a chill.
But then the doc got her a pill,
and Bess had a kiss for Bill.

SUBSTEP 1.5

Sam and Dan

Dan sat in his van.
He had a hot bun with jam.
"Yum! Yum!" said Dan.

"Is that all you have?"
said his chum, Sam.

"What do you have?" said Dan.

"I have ham in the can,
fish in a tin,
and egg nog in a jug.
Have some!" said Sam.

"I will pass," said Dan.

On the Path

Tim huffs and Jim puffs
on the path that
zigs and zags.

The kids lug packs
on their backs
and this is what they have:
Beds and kits,
Balls and mitts,
Nuts and chips,
Subs and sips.

"Let's sit," said Tim.
"Let's nap," said Jim.
"Not yet."
"Why not?"
"It's hot."
"Let's sup."
"Yup, yup!"

Hank, the King

Hank, the king, just had to sing.
He sang a long, long song.

Then Hank saw a ship begin to sink.
"What can I do? I have to think!"

Then, with a bang,
Hank sang and sang and sang.

His song was a tip to the men in the ship,
and the men in the bunks got up.

Honk! went a tug as it did lug
and yank the ship to the bank.

The bell on the ship then did ring
to thank Hank, the singing king!

Hank, in his mink,
could only wink
and sing a long, long song.

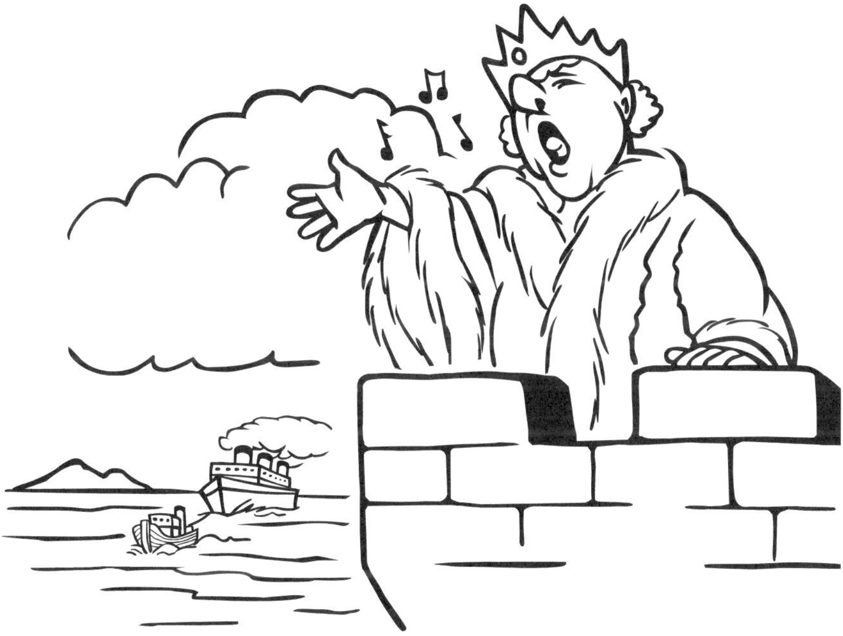

The Run

Fran and Stan held a test
just to see who was best.

"I will be the champ," said Stan.
"We will see who wins," said Fran.

Stan said, "I will win. I have a hunch."
Fran said, "If I win, will you get me lunch?"

"Yes, but do not bet on that," said Stan.
"I am up to the task," said Fran.

The one to snag the flag would win.
The fans did clap and chant and grin.

Well, Stan ran fast but came in last.
Fran got the flag and won a sash.

"You left me in the dust!" said Stan.
"I do not like to brag," said Fran.

"What do you want for lunch?"
"I like hot dogs and punch."

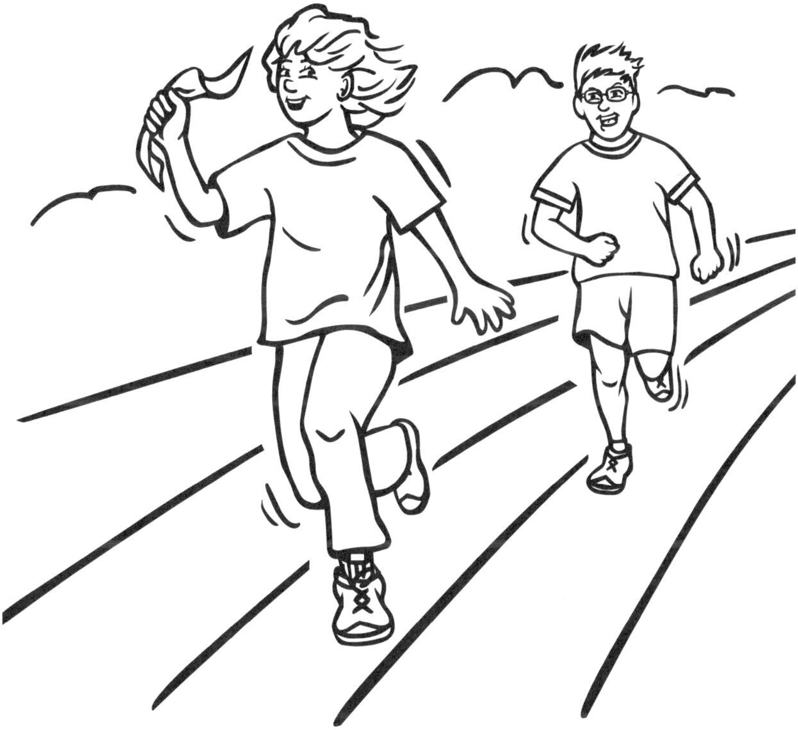

The Small Colt

When Brad was ten years old,
his dad got him a colt.
But when Brad went up to it,
the little colt did bolt.

"Come here, you wild thing!" said Brad.
"I want to hold you, colt."
"You must be kind to him," said Dad.
"You must not scold this colt."

"I will bind him to this post,
and then you must be bold.
If he will not let you pet him,
then he must be sold."

Brad went up to the colt.
"Can I pet you? Do you mind?"
He then added,
"Will you let me, if I am I kind?"

The colt did let Brad pet him,
and it did not seem to mind.
Said Brad, "I have the best small colt
that you will ever find!"

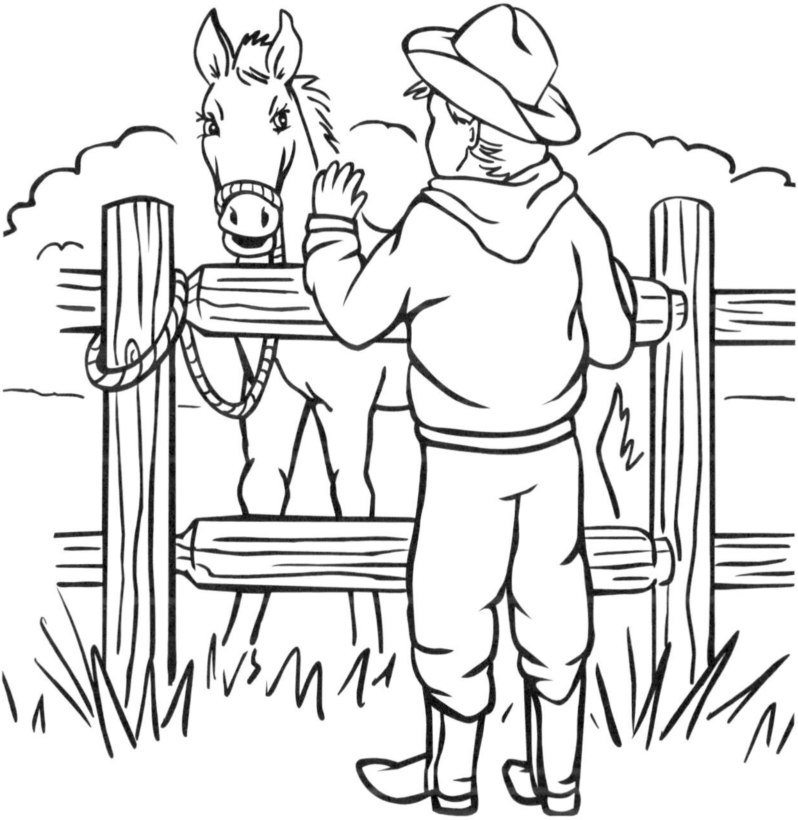

A Grand Plan

Jack squints in the glint of the sun,
and thinks his plan is grand.
He digs up stumps, and grass and clumps,
all from his plot of land.

Jack cuts the trunk of an elm with a slash
and the trunk of an ash on a slant.
These two trunks he then will graft
and that will get him a new plant!

Next, he binds the trunks with a clamp,
and into a trench thrusts the blend.
Jack grunts and stomps. He huffs and stamps,
as the job now comes to an end.

My Cat, Tess

My cat, Tess, gets me full of stress
when she jumps in the trash with a crash.

When I grab her scruff, her fluff is full of stuff.
Hash, and clams, and scraps of scrod!
So off to the bath we plod.

I dunk her in the tub, and scrub, and scrub,
and scrub!

When I let go of her strap,
my wet cat springs to my lap.

"Scram!" I yell, and off she splits.
Then where do I find her?
In my ham and grits!

Seven Small Kittens

Seven small kittens sat in a kennel,
and they made such a racket!
"I must get you some fish to stop all of this,"
Justin said as he got his jacket.

He came back with his pockets full to the brim
with shellfish, and catfish, too.
"I will make a fish sandwich," he told the small kittens.
"Just for me and all of you."

Justin had a bag in his jacket pocket
which he got out when the picnic was done.
He held it up for the kittens to smell and said,
"With this catnip we will have some fun!"

The seven small kittens all said "Meow!"
as they began to jump and run.

"Meow," they all said again and again,
and they did have such fun in the sun!

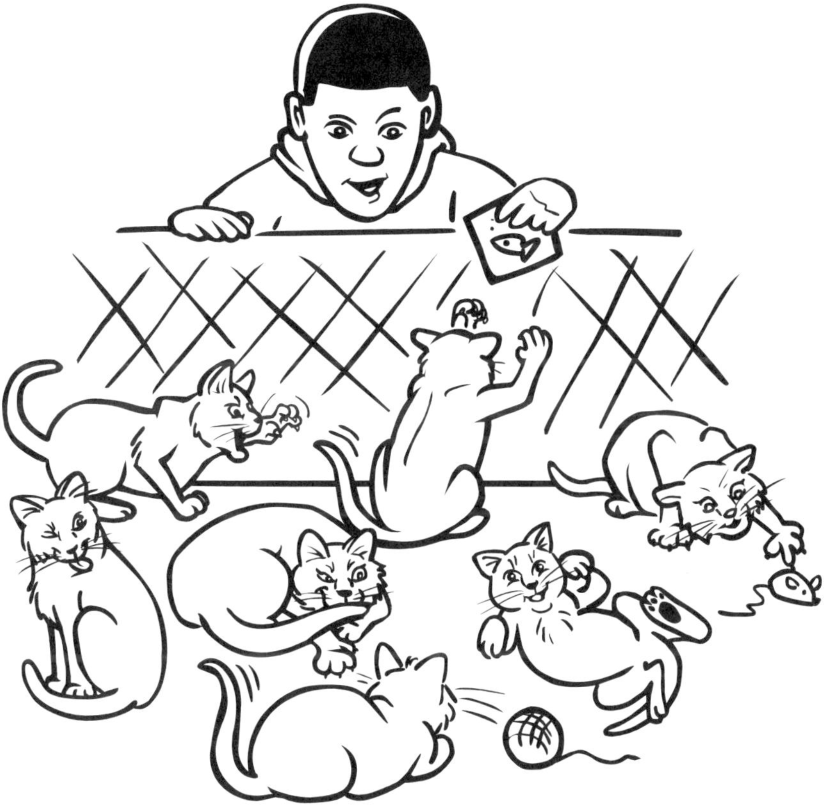

The Dentist

Patrick had a bad tooth
and his mom was frantic.
"We must go to the dentist,
and you must not panic."

Dr. Alfred, the dentist, said,
"I will have to drill it.
And when that is done,
I will have to fill it."

Then Patrick had a tantrum,
and it did not stop
until his mom said he could have
a hundred gumdrops.

"Gumdrops are the problem!"
Dr. Alfred said.
"I must insist you have
something else instead."

Then Patrick said, "What do you have for me?"
and Dr. Alfred said, "Now let me see…
spinach, a salad, a sandwich,"
he said with a grin.
Patrick was upset because
he felt he could not win.

"How about a pretzel?"
Patrick said, "Very well."

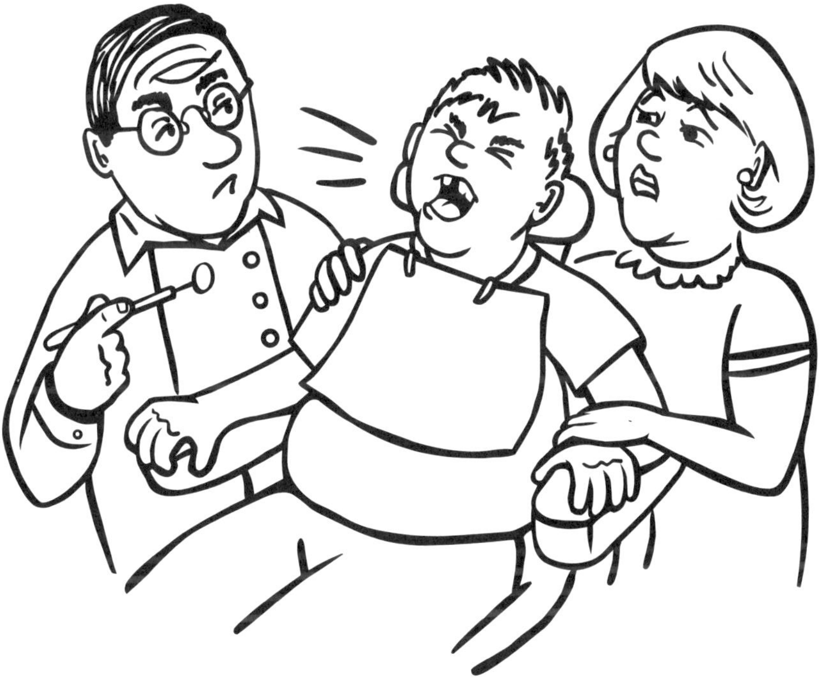

The Class Trip

"The object of this trip is to collect insects.
First, we will collect them.
Then, we will inspect them,"
Mr. Tillis told the class.

"How will we find them?" Shelton asked.
Mr. Tillis said, "Our prospects will be good
if we do as we should.
Class, what should we do?"

The children said,
"Do not run—walk!"
"Do not talk!"
"Look all around!"
"Look up and down!"
"Let nothing distract you!"

Kristen said, "What kinds of insects
can we expect to find?"

"Many kinds, I suspect.
Class, help me with this subject."

The children said:
"Ants!"
"Slugs!"
"Ticks!"
"Moths!"
"Grubs!"
"Maybe even stinkbugs!"

"Yes, yes," said Mr. Tillis.
"Let us go collect them,
and then we will inspect them."

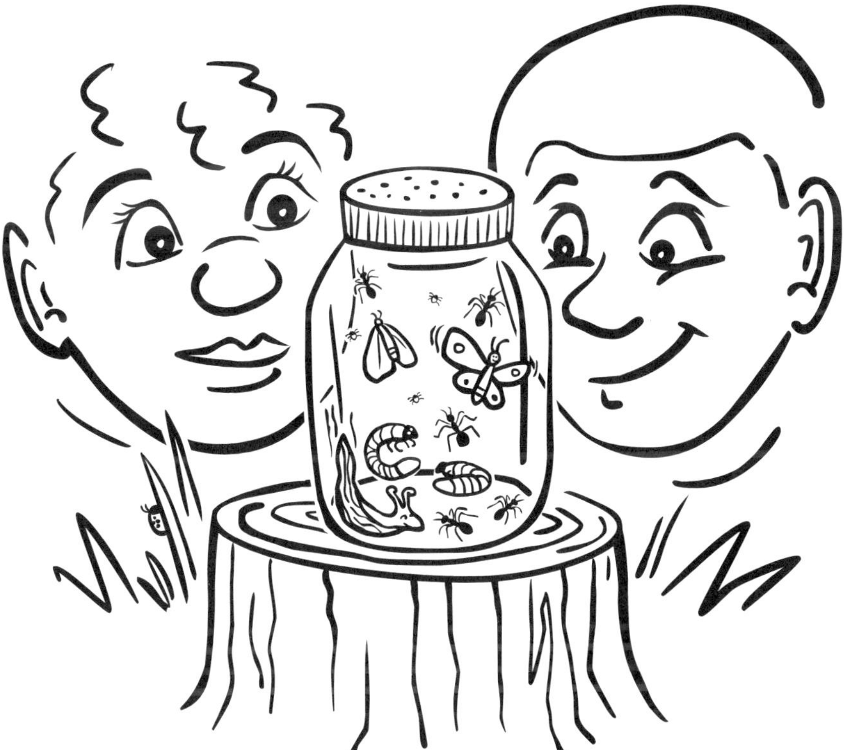

Fantastic Janet

Janet is athletic,
strong, and tall,
and she is a champ
at basketball.

"I recommend
that you see Janet play!"
everyone who sees her
often will say.

Her team travels by bus
to Wisconsin,
Wilmington, Hopkinton,
and Manhattan.

From out in the West
and to the Atlantic
people all say
that she is fantastic!

Janet—athletic,
strong, and tall—
she is the best champ
in basketball.

Dennis

Dennis was a talented man.
He invented:
    a swinging fan,
    a singing pan,
    tall, standing plants,
    expanding pants
    self-mending socks,
    and shrinking rocks,
    sanding dust for vanishing rust,
    tinted lamps,
    printed stamps,
    folded mats,
    molded hats,
the list is never-ending—
and still more things are pending!

The Bike Ride

Mike, Jane, Steve, June, Kate, and Jake
rode their bikes along the lake.

Mike said, "The lane is not too wide."
June said, "Let us ride side by side."

Steve said, "Shall we have a chase?"
June said "No, it is not safe."

Kate said, "Shall we go five miles?"
Jake said, "Let us rest for awhile."

Mike said, "Do we have the time
for a drink of this lemon-lime?"

Jane said, "Yes, and we can take
some grapes and have a bite of cake."

After they all had a small rest,
they rode along with vim and zest.

Up the hills and down the slopes,
they rode in a line,
and when they were close to home,

"Goodbye!" they said with waves and smiles.
"That ride was so, so fine!"

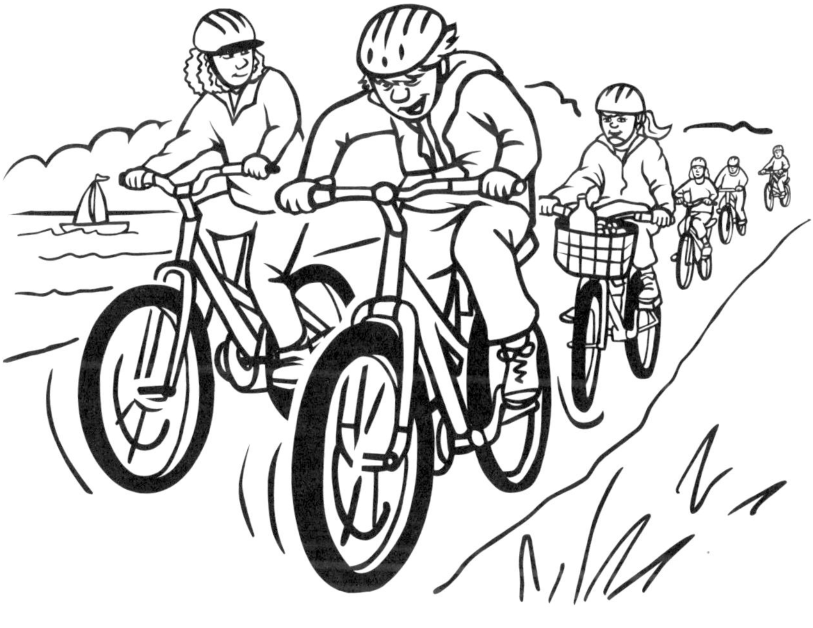

Camping in the Pinelands

Mr. Valdez and Mr. Wineland
took their sons to camp in the Pinelands.

They woke at sunrise and made pancakes,
and then went swimming in a man-made lake.

They saw some wildlife when they took a hike,
and then went fishing for bass and pike.

A king-size fish was on their line—
the fish was big and oh so fine!

They made a campfire and sat to eat.
Then cupcakes made the day complete.

Custom-Made Valentines

Clare wanted custom-made valentines.
She said, "No one will have ones like mine.

I will illustrate them with a rose in red.
I will make them so fine," she said.

"My valentines will not be infantile,
and they will not end up in the trash pile.

The teacher will distribute the valentines,
and the kids will recognize which ones are mine."

"How did you make them?" they will contemplate.
I will ask, "Would you like me to demonstrate?"

Custom-made valentines from Clare
will indicate that she did care.

The Dog Show

The dogs were captive in their crates.
The buzz was buzzing among classmates.
The dog show is at school today!

Which dog will get the blue ribbon?
This is what the kids have to say:

"My dog is expensive!"
"My dog is attentive!"
"My dog is expressive!"
"My dog is active!"
"My dog is massive!"

"Hush!" said the teacher,
then got up with a wink.
"I can give each one
a ribbon, I think."

A ribbon for all the impressive dogs:
the expensive dog
the attentive dog
the expressive dog
the active dog
and last but not least
a ribbon for the massive dog.

The dogs were again captive in their crates.
The buzz was still buzzing among the classmates.

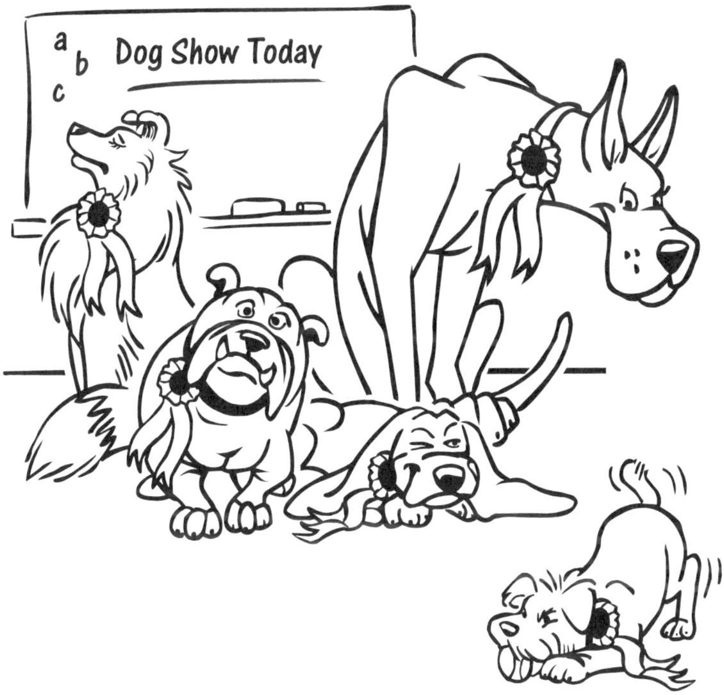
a
b
c
Dog Show Today

The Tennis Pro

My gram, Flo, is a tennis pro.
When she hits the ball,
we all want to know, "Where did it go?"

I see it fly by in the sky.
"Just tell me how you do it, Gram.
Tell me, Gram," I cry.

Gram said, "I am good, if I may say so,
and I will tell you why,
for I am not at all shy.

I never say no to a game of tennis,
for tennis keeps me spry.
And if you want to be good at something,
you must try and try and try."

The Best Hotel

"Hello! My name is Mr. Coleman.
I am calling to request a room."

"Well, Mr. Coleman, I declare,
of all the hotels, you have selected well."

"Can you tell me why?"

The man said, "Yes, but where shall I begin?

When you come into our hotel,
we will prepare what you like.
Our food is fresh, not frozen,
and the moment it is done, we will bring it up to you.

With a click of your remote,
you can find any program on TV.
We have hundreds of channels,
and you can find a game you like to see.

I predict that you will relax
when you smell lilacs beside your bed.
And with the press of a button,
you can have a fire, then retire—
content and well-fed.

"A refund on your next visit
will be given to you as an added bonus.
We will not neglect your demands.
We respond in an instant—not one thing will we miss!"

Mr. Coleman said, "You are so polite.
My visits will be frequent—on that you can depend.
You have spoken to me with such respect,
your hotel will be one that I will recommend."

The Pet Rally

Sandy had a funny puppy.
The puppy's name was Penny.
Billy had a silly kitty.
The kitty's name was Kenny.
Tony had a tiny guppy.
The guppy's name was Freddy.
Amy had a pretty pony.
The pony's name was Teddy.
Molly had a fuzzy bunny.
The bunny's name was Missy.
And Henry had a skinny snake.
The skinny snake was Sissy.

The kids had a rally
one fine and sunny day,
and they chose to let their pets
come outside to play.

The pets were unruly
and they ran away.
"Golly! What a folly!"
That's what I have to say!

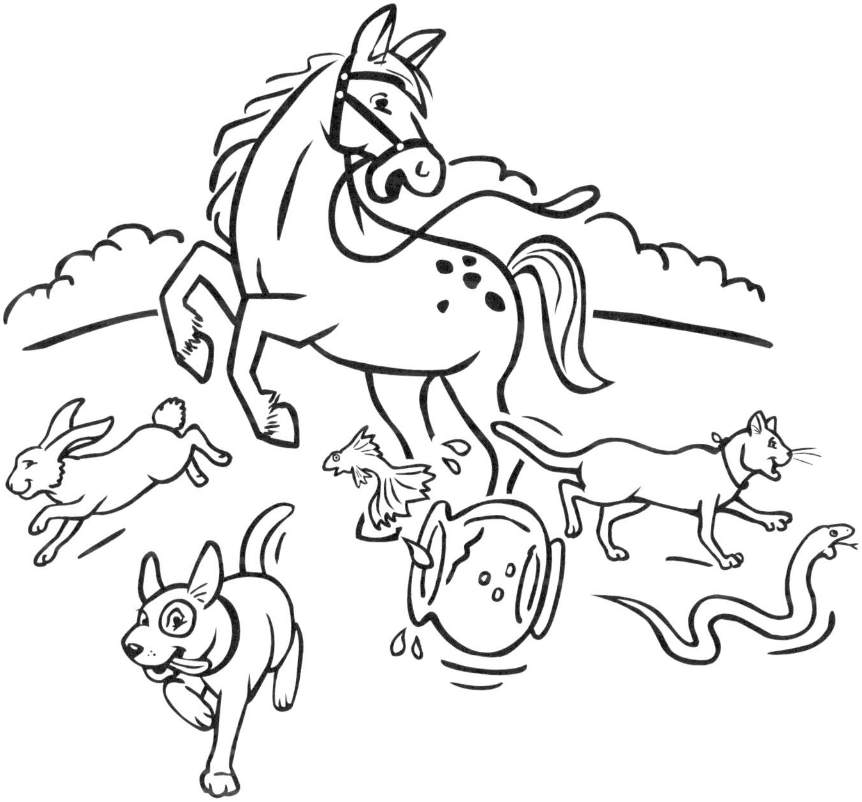

One Day Long Ago

One day long ago, my father said to me:

"Do you wish to comprehend the galaxy?
Overcome your opponent or enemy?

Develop a cure with a microscope?
Travel down a volcano on a rope?

Play a melody on an instrument?
Camp by yourself in the wild in a tent?

Prepare a white coconut wedding cake?
Immunize children whose lives are at stake?

You can do anything you want to do
if you stay in school and follow the rules.
Your teachers are there to educate you.

Be polite and do not disrespect.
Just smile, say thank you, and use your intellect."

Donna Apollo

When Donna Apollo gave her class address,
she said, "Friends, do not hesitate to vote for me,
for I alone will give you more—not less!

You will get extra time to study,
and take your exams with your best buddy.

Vanilla milkshakes at lunchtime
will be sold for a dime!

We will have a domino contest each day
along with many other games we can play.

Students, it is not difficult to see
that the very best candidate to vote for is me!

There can be no substitute, I am confident.
Elect me, Donna Apollo, for class president!"

Mrs. Yang

Mrs. Yang is frequently on the street
selling her wares to those that she meets.

She sings:
"I have lumpy crab cakes and lots of shellfish.
Get a plateful to share—do not be selfish!

Have a plate of crispy fish and chips
or some hot and crunchy chicken strips.

I have cheese from the strongest to the mildest
and yummy grapes—the sweetest and the wildest."

Her refreshments are impressive—
you must visit her stand.
Her things are not too costly,
and I think they are just grand!

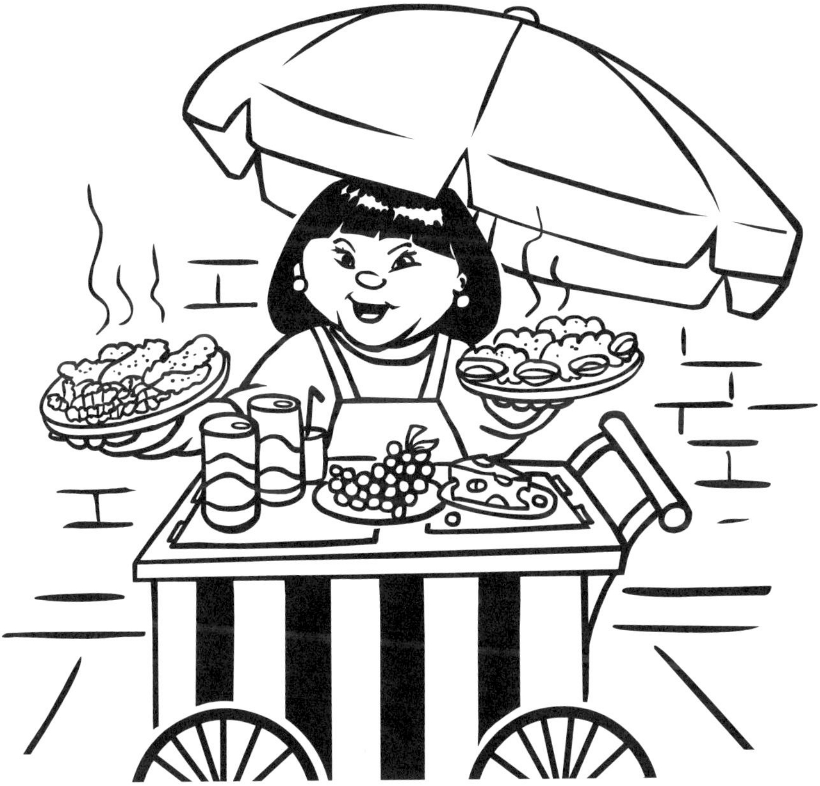

Wendy

Wendy had to baby-sit
the kids called Mick and Vin.
It was a job that stressed her,
for she felt she could not win.

When their mom and dad were gone,
the kids rushed off to play,
and they would not do anything
that Wendy had to say.

They smashed and bashed.
They jumped and bumped.
They banged and clanged.
They huffed and puffed.

"Get undressed!" Wendy called
as she filled the tub.
In they dashed. Then they splashed.
Wendy rubbed and scrubbed.

When they were dressed, she was drenched,
and she tossed them into bed,
lulled them to sleep with a song,
and kissed them on the head.

Wishfulness

"Do you have a willingness to work?"
the man at the shop asked me.
"I will work very willingly,"
I responded respectfully.

"Is helpfulness something you possess?"
"Helpfulness is my best quality!"
I responded expressively.

"Can you work skillfully and tirelessly?"
"Just give me a try and you will see,"
I responded hopefully.

"You conduct yourself impressively.
And the job is yours," he said trustfully.
"Thank you!" I responded gratefully.

Dapple-Gray Nag

When he is able,
Johnny goes to the stable
to see his dapple-gray nag.

Her name is Nelly.
She loves apples with jelly
that she nibbles from his bag.

She starts to snuffle,
then begins to scuffle,
as Johnny comes with the tack.

When she is idle,
Johnny puts on her bridle,
then the saddle upon her back.

Over land they ramble.
Up and down they scramble.

In puddles they wade,
with maples for shade.

Through thistles that bristle,
they hear the wind whistle.

Then suddenly, down comes the rain!
So they huddle and nestle
by a railroad trestle,
then amble on home down the lane.

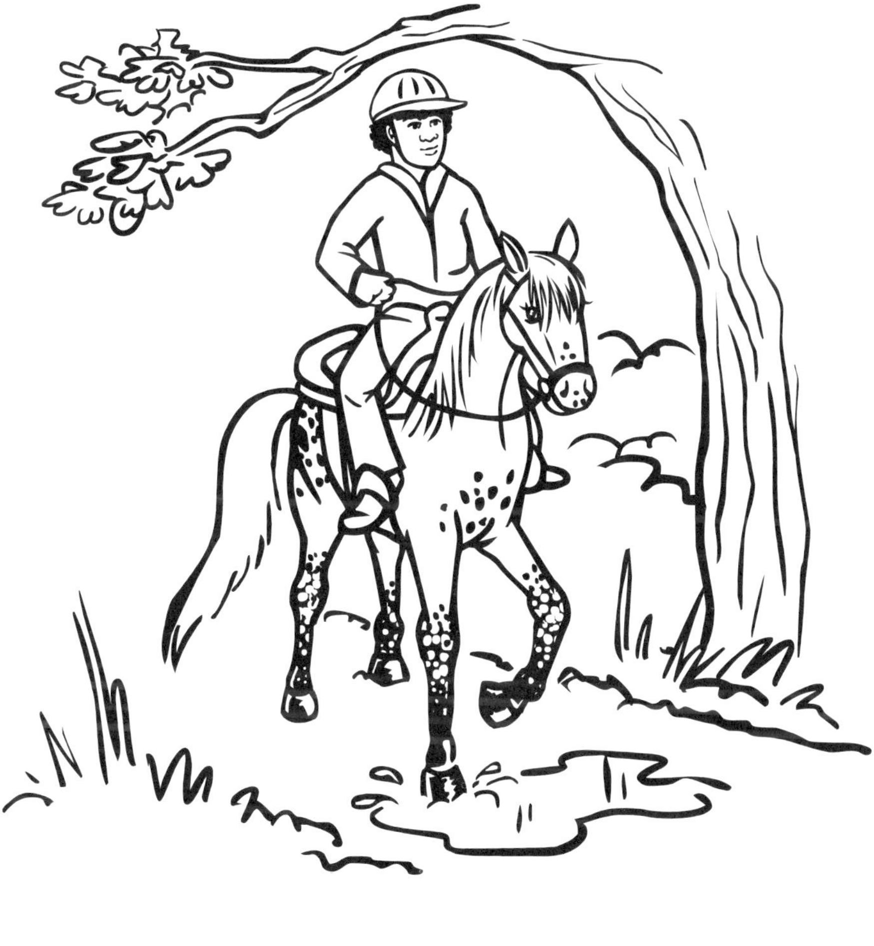

Fundations Alignment

This table lists the Fundations level and unit in which the language concept presented in the poem is first introduced.

Poem	Page	Level 1	Level 2	Level 3
The Fat Rat	1	Unit 2	Unit 1	Unit 1
Zag	3	Unit 3	Unit 1	Unit 1
No Fish!	5	Unit 3	Unit 1	Unit 1
Bess and Bill	7	Unit 4	Unit 2	Unit 1
Sam and Dan	7	Unit 5	Unit 2	Unit 1
On the Path	8	Unit 6	Unit 2	Unit 1
Hank, the King	9	Unit 7	Unit 2	Unit 1
The Run	11	Unit 8	Unit 1	Unit 1
The Small Colt	13	N/A	Unit 3	Unit 1
A Grand Plan	15	Unit 8	Unit 2	Unit 1
My Cat, Tess	16	Unit 8	Unit 1	Unit 1
Seven Small Kittens	17	Unit 11	Unit 5	Unit 3
The Dentist	19	Unit 11	Unit 5	Unit 3
The Class Trip	21	N/A	N/A	N/A
Fantastic Janet	23	N/A	Unit 5	Unit 3
Dennis	24	Unit 13	Unit 5	Unit 3
The Bike Ride	25	Unit 14	Unit 6	Unit 3
Camping in the Pinelands	27	N/A	Unit 6	Unit 3
Custom-Made Valentines	28	N/A	Unit 6	Unit 3
The Dog Show	29	N/A	Unit 6	Unit 5
The Tennis Pro	31	N/A	Unit 7	Unit 6
The Best Hotel	32	N/A	Unit 7	Unit 6
The Pet Rally	33	N/A	Unit 7	Unit 6
One Day Long Ago	35	N/A	Unit 7	Unit 6
Donna Apollo	36	N/A	N/A	Unit 6
Mrs. Yang	37	N/A	Unit 7	Unit 6
Wendy	39	N/A	Unit 7	Unit 2
Wishfulness	40	N/A	N/A	N/A
Dapple-Gray Nag	41	N/A	Unit 7	Unit 8